PERSPECTIVES 2000

TESTS

LINDA LEE

Intermediate English 1 & 2

Heinle & Heinle Publishers
A Division of Wadsworth, Inc.
Boston Massachusetts 02116 U.S.A.

CONTENTS

Introduction 1

Achievement Tests

    Book 1, Test A (Units 1-3) 2

    Book 1, Test B (Units 4-6) 8

    Book 1, Test C (Units 7-9) 15

    Book 2, Test A (Units 1-3) 21

    Book 2, Test B (Units 4-6) 28

    Book 2, Test C (Units 7-9) 35

    Test Scripts and Answer Keys 42

Copyright © 1992
by Heinle & Heinle Publishers,
A Division of Wadsworth, Inc.
under the Universal Copyright Convention,
International Copyright Convention, and
Pan-American Copyright Convention.

This material may be reproduced for use in the classroom.

Manufactured in the United States of America

ISBN 0-8384-2222-5

10 9 8 7 6 5 4 3 2

INTRODUCTION

This volume contains the six achievement tests for *Perspectives 2000,* Books 1 and 2. These tests are designed to be given in the following intervals:

> Book 1: Test A after finishing Units 1-3
> Book 1: Test B after finishing Units 4-6
> Book 1: Test C after finishing Units 7-9
>
> Book 2: Test A after finishing Units 1-3
> Book 2: Test B after finishing Units 4-6
> Book 2: Test C after finishing Units 7-9

Each achievement test covers the functional and grammatical structures presented in the specified units. Students can score a maximum of 100 points on each test.

Allow approximately 50 minutes of class time for each test. Begin the test by reading the listening script, which can be found on pages 42-61. Students can complete the rest of the test at their own pace.

When reading the listening scripts, alter your voice to represent the different characters speaking. As an alternative, you may wish to tape-record the scripts with the assistance of one or two associates to add realism to the dialogues.

It is highly recommended that the achievement tests be used in conjunction with other process-oriented evaluation strategies when assessing student progress. These strategies could include the following:

- **Systematic observation.** Systematically make notes on students' performance during class. Observations should include things that students do well and areas that need work. These notes can be organized in a notebook for later reference.

- **Recordings.** Make audio or video tapes of students talking in class and working together. Students can listen to or watch the tapes and discuss their progress with you.

- **Portfolios.** Have students date their written work and keep it in a portfolio. Periodically review their work to note areas of improvement and areas that still need work.

- **Interviews.** In both formal and informal settings, give students the opportunity to talk about their progress with the language and their response to classroom activities.

NAME: _____ DATE: _____ Book 1
Test A
Units 1-3

PART 1 (10 points)

QUESTIONS 1-5: You will hear five short conversations between two speakers. At the end of each conversation, you will hear a question. Read the answers on your test paper and circle the letter of the best answer. You will hear the conversation and question two times.

Listen to the following example.

You will hear:
    Woman: *Have you been waiting long?*
    Man: *No, I just got here a few minutes ago.*
    Third Voice: *How long has the man been waiting for the woman?*

You will read:
    A. For a long time.
    B. For just a few minutes.
    C. A few minutes ago.
    D. In a while.

From the conversation you know that the correct answer is *B*. Now get ready to listen to the five conversations.

1. A. Right away.
   B. Already.
   C. Later.
   D. A long time ago.

2. A. He wants her to call him.
   B. He wants a telephone call.
   C. He wants her to call them.
   D. She wants to call them.

3. A. She's going to fill out the questionnaire.
   B. She didn't do it.
   C. She hasn't asked a question yet.
   D. She hasn't filled out the questionnaire yet.

4. A. They were sleeping.
   B. They are listening to music.
   C. They are feeling tired.
   D. They were listening to music.

5. A. He forgot to make dinner.
   B. He invited her to dinner.
   C. He forgot to invite Mark for dinner.
   D. He is always forgetting about dinner.

PART 2 (20 points)

QUESTIONS 6-15: Complete the conversations. On the blank lines, write the correct tense and form of the verbs in parentheses.

6. A: How did you do on the test?

   B: I didn't have any trouble (answer) _____ the questions, so I think I did well.

7. A: Are you a morning person or a night person?

   B: I guess I'm a morning person. I usually (get up) _____ early.

8. A: Do you ever get drowsy during the day?

   B: Sometimes I (get) _____ drowsy in the afternoon.

9. A: What's wrong? You look upset.

   B: I'm not upset. I'm just nervous about (take) _____ this exam.

10. A: How was your vacation?

    B: Terrible. Whenever I (go) _____ on vacation, I get sick.

11. A: What were you doing when I called?

    B: I (watch) _____ something on TV.

12. A: What did you have for lunch?

    B: I didn't have time for lunch. In fact, I (not/eat) _____ anything since breakfast.

13. A: Joshua, have you seen Michi today?

    B: Yes, I have. I saw him while I (walk) _____ to school.

14. A: Do you know Lucas Rindler?

    B: Of course I do. I (know) _____ him for years.

15. A: Are you ready to leave?

    B: I'm ready but Nick isn't. He (sleep) _____.

BOOK 1: TEST A

PART 3 (20 points)

QUESTIONS 16-25: On the lines below, write the correct tense and form of the verbs in parentheses.

16. The telephone (ring) _____. Could you please answer it?

17. Last year I (not/have) _____ time to take a vacation, but this year I hope to take a long trip.

18. We eat outside whenever the weather (be) _____ nice.

19. A person's blood pressure (change) _____ over a twenty-four hour period.

20. I went to a terrible movie last night. It (be) _____ the worst movie I have ever seen.

21. My parents have finished building their house, but they (not/move) _____ in yet.

22. I think that I'm finally getting used to (live) _____ in the city.

23. My uncle invited me (go) _____ with him, but I had to refuse.

24. I (see) _____ my cousin next month.

25. I would like (see) _____ the largest suitcase that you have.

PART 4 (10 points)

QUESTIONS 26-30. Each of the following sentences has a word or phrase underlined. Below each sentence are four other words or phrases. Choose the word or phrase that keeps the meaning of the original sentence. Circle the letter of your answer.

26. The water rose gradually.
    A. quickly   B. suddenly   C. slowly   D. unexpectedly

27. She gave the cue to stand up.
    A. signal   B. answer   C. routine   D. routine

28. Has it been filled out yet?
    A. repaired   B. sent   C. received   D. completed

29. This is confidential information.
    A. important   B. unusual   C. strange   D. private

30. His story is ridiculous.
    A. unfair   B. silly   C. unpleasant   D. true

PART 5 (20 points)

QUESTIONS 31-40. Complete the sentences below with the correct form of the word in parentheses.

Dear Ricardo,

As soon as I (get) _____ your letter yesterday, I
                              31
called Jean and Mike to tell them your news. We will miss you, but I'm

glad that you have decided (stay) _____ there until the
                                         32
end of summer.

Things (be) _____ pretty quiet here now. Classes
                 33
(end) _____ two weeks ago, and since then I (look)
          34
_____ for a summer job. Jean and Mike already
       35
(have) _____ jobs, so I don't get to see them very much.
           36
Mike seems a lot (happy) _____ now that he is working.
                                    37

Write to us whenever you (feel) _____ homesick.
                                             38
I'll write and I'll encourage Mike (write) _____ too.
                                                  39
Please don't get accustomed (live) _____ there. We all
                                              40
want you to come back soon.

Take care,

Laura

PART 6 (20 points)

QUESTIONS 41-45: Read the passage and answer the questions. Circle the best answer.

From its beginning in 1790, the U.S. decennial census has been more than a simple "headcount." Gathering information on sex and age in its first census, the government was able to get definite knowledge about the military and industrial strength of the country. Since then, the size, composition, and distribution of the population have changed—and with them, the need for statistical information. *To stay in step* with these changes, the content of the census has varied over time. Since 1940, the decennial census has asked questions about population and housing.

While the Census Bureau, founded in 1902, is well known for the national Census of Population and Housing taken every 10 years, the agency also conducts national agriculture, economic, and government censuses every five years. Besides censuses, the Census Bureau administers about 250 sample surveys each year. These data-collection efforts result in thousands of statistical reports each year. All of this has earned the Census Bureau the name "Factfinder for the Nation."

41. What is the subject of the first paragraph?

    A. How the census has changed.
    B. The census today.
    C. The population of the United States today.
    D. The size of the Census Bureau.

42. Which of these facts is **not** included in the passage?

    A. The year of the first census.
    B. The content of today's census.
    C. The number of questions on a census form.
    D. The age of the Census Bureau.

43. In the first paragraph, the italicized phrase *to stay in step* probably means to

    A. depend on.
    B. keep up with.
    C. understand.
    D. fill out.

44. Which of the following statements is true according to the passage?

    A. The Census Bureau has existed for fewer than fifty years.
    B. The first U.S. census did not ask questions about age.
    C. The first U.S. census took place in 1790.
    D. The Census Bureau conducts censuses, but it does not get involved in doing surveys.

45. What is the subject of the second paragraph?

    A. The varied work of the Census Bureau.
    B. The early years of the Census Bureau.
    C. The Census of Population and Housing.
    D. Who works at the Census Bureau.

BOOK 1: TEST A

NAME: _____ DATE: _____   Book 1
                                                    Test B
                                                    Units 4-6

PART 1 (10 points)

QUESTIONS 1-5: You are going to hear five sentences. You will hear each sentence two times. Choose the sentence on your test paper that is closest in meaning or identical in meaning. Circle the letter of that sentence.

   Listen to the example. You will hear: *John's not present in class today.*
   You will read:
           A. The class didn't give John a gift.
           B. Today John has a presentation to do in class.
           C. John is absent from class.
           D. John's not the president of his class.

The correct answer is *C.* Sentence C has the same meaning as the sentence you heard, "John's not present in class today." Now get ready to listen to the five sentences.

1. A. He was the right person for the job.
   B. He was qualified to do the job, but he didn't get it.
   C. He didn't get the job because he wasn't qualified.
   D. He can't get a job because he doesn't have any qualifications.

2. A. You cannot graduate if you pass this course.
   B. If you don't pass this course, you won't graduate.
   C. You don't have to take this course to graduate.
   D. After you graduate, you will have to take this course.

3. A. I will tell you her name if you want to know it.
   B. If you don't know her name, I will tell you.
   C. I know her name, but I am not supposed to tell you.
   D. I don't know her name, so I can't tell you.

4. A. You are required to do that.
   B. You should do that.
   C. You shouldn't do that.
   D. You must do that.

5. A. It is possible that I will be late because I must go to the store.
   B. If I go to the store, I will be late.
   C. If I am late, I will go to the store.
   D. I must not be late because I have to go to the store.

PART 2 (10 points)

QUESTIONS 6-10: You will hear five short conversations between two speakers. At the end of each conversation, you will hear a question. Read the answers on your test paper and circle the letter of the best answer. You will hear the conversation and question two times

Listen to the following example.

You will hear:

    Woman: *Have you been waiting long?*
    Man: *No, I just got here a few minutes ago.*
    Third Voice: *How long has the man been waiting?*

You will read:
- A. For a long time.
- B. For just a few minutes.
- C. A few minutes ago.
- D. In a while.

From the conversation you know that the correct answer is *B*. Now get ready to listen to the five conversations.

6.
    - A. In a movie theater.
    - B. At a party.
    - C. In a store.
    - D. In a restaurant.

7.
    - A. He should take the test on Friday.
    - B. He shouldn't take the test.
    - C. He should study tonight.
    - D. He might not do very well on the test.

8.
    - A. He is supposed to call Jim.
    - B. Jim is supposed to wait by the phone.
    - C. He is supposed to wait for the woman.
    - D. He is supposed to wait by the phone.

9.
    - A. Taking a job.
    - B. Quitting a job.
    - C. How to do a job.
    - D. When to start a job.

10.
    - A. It's not very good.
    - B. She doesn't like it.
    - C. The beginning is not very good, but it gets better.
    - D. She doesn't want to continue reading it.

PART 3 (10 points)

QUESTIONS 11-15: Complete these conversations with *must, must not,* or *don't (doesn't) have to.* Write your answers on the blank lines.

11. A: What time does the party start?

    B: It's supposed to start at eight.

    A: Really? Then we _____ leave here by seven-thirty in order to get there on time.

12. A: I hear that you're thinking of buying a new car.

    B: Well, I _____ buy one right away because my old car is working fine. But I'm looking around for a new one.

13. A: You _____ tell anyone that today is my birthday.

    B: Why not?

    A: I don't want anyone to sing *Happy Birthday.*

14. A: This is the slowest restaurant I've ever been to. We've been sitting here for an hour and we still haven't gotten anything to eat.

    B: We _____ stay here. If you want to go, let's go.

15. A: You're going to be late for school. You'd better get going.

    B: Didn't I tell you? I _____ go to school today. It's a holiday.

PART 4 (10 points)

QUESTIONS 16-20: In each of the following sentences, one of the four underlined parts is wrong. Write the letter of the wrong part in the blank. IMPORTANT: Do not correct the wrong part of the sentence; just write the letter in the blank.

Example: _C_   <u>Last week</u> John <u>got</u> on the bus and went to his <u>sister</u> new
                       A   B   C
apartment to visit <u>her</u>.
                              D

The correct answer is *C.* The underlined word *sister* is incorrect.

_____ 16. If you want to stay later, I come back to pick you up.
       A   B C   D

_____ 17. If you don't listen carefully, you might not hearing the date of the exam.
     A   B   C   D

_____ 18. My brother and sister have been living with my uncle since December
    A   B   C

    because my parents were on a trip.
           D

_____ 19. My brother's restaurant has become very popular since it has opened
    A   B   C

    three months ago.
         D

_____ 20. How would you feeling if a good friend stopped speaking or writing to
      A   B   C   D

    you?

PART 5 (10 points)

QUESTIONS 21-25: Complete the sentences below with *have to, must not,* or *don't (doesn't) have to.* Write your answers on the blank lines.

21. When the instructor sees two people talking during the written exam, he says,

 "You _____ talk during the exam."

22. Five-year-old Kamal runs out into the street. His mother runs after him and

 says, "You _____ run out into the street."

23. Sarah usually gives Maya a ride to work. Today, however, Maya is going to drive her own car to work. Maya calls Sarah and says,

 "You _____ give me a ride today."

24. Maria is taking an evening course to study English. When her friend Leila

 invites her for dinner, she says, "I can't. I _____ go to class tonight."

25. Tyler usually leaves for school at 8 a.m. Today at 8 a.m. he is still eating his breakfast. His mother says, "You are going to be late. You

 _____ leave right away."

PART 6 (10 points)

QUESTIONS 26-30: Complete the sentences below with the modal *must, should,* or *might*. Write your answers on the blank lines.

26. Your friend has been driving for many hours. You say, "You

    _____ be tired. Why don't you let me drive for awhile?"

27. Your friend has a headache. You say to him, "You _____ probably lie down for a while."

28. When you look out the window, you see that people are wearing heavy coats.

    You think to yourself, "It _____ be cold outside today."

29. Your shoes hurt your feet. You say to yourself, "I _____ get rid of these shoes. They are too small."

30. You invite a friend to travel with you during the summer. She says, "I'm

    thinking of taking a computer course this summer, so I _____ have to stay here this summer."

PART 7 (10 points)

QUESTIONS 31-35: Read each pair of sentences below. Use the information in the first sentence to complete the second sentence. Write your answers on the blank lines.

31. Carlos isn't getting very good grades in school because he doesn't study very much.

    If he _____ harder, he _____ better grades.

32. On rainy days Serena takes the bus to school.

    If it _____ today, she _____ the bus.

33. Tom can't hear the telephone because he is working downstairs.

    If he _____ downstairs now, he _____ the telephone.

34. Theo can't mail the package because the post office is closed.

    If the post office _____ closed, he _____ the package.

35. Celia can't get a teaching job because she doesn't have a Ph.D.

    If she _____ a Ph.D., she _____ a teaching job.

PART 8 (10 points)

QUESTIONS 36-40: Each of the following sentences has a word or phrase underlined. Below each sentence are four other words or phrases. Choose the word or phrase that keeps the meaning of the original sentence. Circle the letter of your answer.

36. It was a delightful trip.
    A. dangerous   B. helpful   C. strange   D. pleasant

37. This course is mandatory.
    A. easy   B. required   C. enjoyable   D. unnecessary

38. Why did you give up?
    A. stop trying   B. refuse   C. obey   D. survive

39. The two cars crashed.
    A. raced   B. drove away   C. ran into each other   D. stopped

40. He performed many tasks.
    A. duties   B. qualifications   C. launches   D. orbits

PART 9 (20 points)

Read the passage and answer the questions. Circle your answers.

If you are interested in the field of law, you might want to consider a career as a lawyer or a legal assistant. In the United States, the demand for these professionals is increasing. In fact, the field of legal assistants is one of the ten fastest-growing occupations in the United States.

What does it take to enter the legal profession? If you want to become a lawyer in most states, you must first complete four years of undergraduate study in a college or university. While in college, you should take courses in a variety of areas; you do not have to take law courses at this time. After finishing your undergraduate studies, you must then complete three years of law school. In law school, you will have to take required courses on topics such as contracts, criminal law, and property. In your second and third years of law school, however, you may choose specialized courses in your area of interest. Once you have graduated from law school, you are still not ready to practice law. You must be admitted to the bar of the state in which you want to practice law. In order to be admitted to the bar, you must take a written examination. If you pass the examination, you can practice law in that state.

If you are interested in the profession of law, but you do not want to spend so many years in school, you might consider becoming a legal assistant. Legal assistants research laws and do the background work for a lawyer. In fact, legal assistants do much of the routine work that lawyers used to do. To become a legal assistant, you do not have to have formal training. However, most employers prefer to hire someone who has completed a special academic program. These programs can last from one to three years and are offered by four-year colleges and universities as well as private business schools. To get into some legal assistant programs, you must already have a bachelor's degree. For other programs, a college education is not required.

41. What is the topic of the second paragraph?

   A. The qualifications for becoming a lawyer and a legal assistant.
   B. The qualifications for becoming a lawyer.
   C. The qualifications for becoming a legal assistant.
   D. Occupations in the United States.

42. Which of these statements is true based on the reading?

   A. To become a lawyer, you must take law courses for four years.
   B. You can practice law as soon as you finish law school.
   C. Once you take the bar examination, you can practice in any state.
   D. You must complete your undergraduate studies before you can enter law school.

43. Leila is in her first year of law school. She says,

   A. "I haven't finished my undergraduate studies yet."
   B. "Next year I'm going to specialize in maritime law."
   C. "Last year I specialized in maritime law."
   D. "I've just taken the bar examination."

44 Unlike lawyers, legal assistants

   A. must go to law school.
   B. do not have to have specialized training.
   C. have to take a bar examination.
   D. must have a bachelor's degree.

45. In the third paragraph, the word *hire* means

   A. get to know.
   B. examine.
   C. give a job to.
   D. give advice to.

NAME: _____ DATE: _____ Book 1
Test C
Units 7-9

PART 1 (20 points)

QUESTIONS 1-10: You are going to hear ten short conversations between two speakers. At the end of each conversation, you will hear a statement. Use the information in the conversation to decide if the statement is true or false. Circle TRUE or FALSE. You will hear the conversation and statement two times.

Listen to the following example.

You will hear:

    Woman: *I found the book that you lost.*
    Man: *Great. Where was it?*
    Woman: *In my car.*
    Third Voice: *True or False? The woman found the man's book.*

From the conversation you know that the correct answer is *True*. Now get ready to listen to the conversations.

1. TRUE   FALSE
2. TRUE   FALSE
3. TRUE   FALSE
4. TRUE   FALSE
5. TRUE   FALSE
6. TRUE   FALSE
7. TRUE   FALSE
8. TRUE   FALSE
9. TRUE   FALSE
10. TRUE   FALSE

BOOK 1: TEST C

PART 2 (10 points)

QUESTIONS 11-15: Use the timeline to complete the sentences that follow. On the blank line, write the correct tense of the verb in parentheses.

Example: Ken (work) __*is working*__ for DECA now.

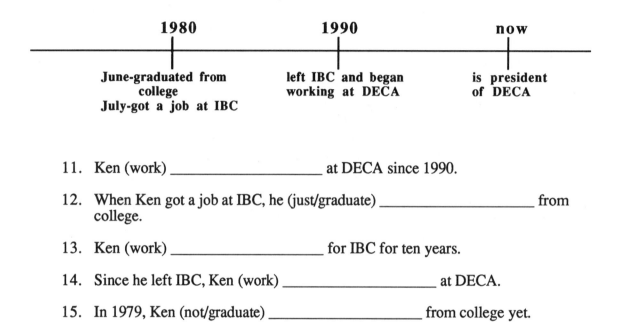

11. Ken (work) _____ at DECA since 1990.

12. When Ken got a job at IBC, he (just/graduate) _____ from college.

13. Ken (work) _____ for IBC for ten years.

14. Since he left IBC, Ken (work) _____ at DECA.

15. In 1979, Ken (not/graduate) _____ from college yet.

PART 3 (10 points)

QUESTIONS 16-20: Complete the sentences on the left with a clause from the list on the right. Write the letter of the clause on the blank line to the left.

_____ 16. The students _____ will not be able to take the test.

_____ 17. Jim _____ broke his leg yesterday.

_____ 18. I can't find the book _____.

_____ 19. The book *Iron and Silk* _____ has been made into a movie.

_____ 20. A friend _____ is coming to visit tonight.

A. who works with me

B. that you gave me

C. who are absent

D. , which is about an American teacher in China,

E. , who works with me,

PART 4 (10 points)

QUESTIONS 21-25: Complete these sentences with the correct form of the verbs in parentheses. Write your answers on the blank lines.

21. It's late. Do you think we can get anyone (come) _____ to fix the heater at this hour?

22. I can ask you to study harder, but I can't make you (do) _____ it.

23. Did you let the dog (go) _____ outside?

24. Can you get someone (move) _____ this table?

25. I think we should have the children (do) _____ the dishes.

PART 5 (10 points)

QUESTIONS 26-30: Add information about a noun or pronoun in each of the sentences below. Use the relative pronoun in parentheses in your new sentence.

Example: The corporation is large. (in which)
   The corporation in which he works is large.

26. On my way home, I met someone. (who)
   _____

27. On my way to school, I talked to someone. (whom)
   _____

28. The letter took three weeks to go from California to Florida. (that)
   _____

29. The woman has moved away. (whose)
   _____

30. The area is unique. (in which)
   _____

BOOK 1: TEST C

PART 6 (10 points)

QUESTIONS 26-35: In each of the following sentences, one of the four underlined parts is wrong. Write the letter of the wrong part in the blank. IMPORTANT: Do not correct the wrong part of the sentence; just write the letter in the blank.

Example: __C__ Last week John got on the bus and went to his sister new
         A   B   C

apartment to visit her.
      D

The correct answer is *C*. The underlined word *sister* is incorrect.

_____ 31. By the time my brother got here, we had already decided going out for
         A   B   C   D

dinner.

_____ 32. If you work steady, you will finish this before the bell rings and you
           A   B   C

have to leave.
 D

_____ 33. One of mine friends has the same name as an actor who is very popular
        A   B   C   D

today.

_____ 34. One of my sister's lives on Pond Street, which is the last street after the
          A   B C   D

library.

_____ 35. We have been talking for several hours when she suddenly told me that
       A   B   C

she was going to get married.
   D

PART 7 (10 points)

QUESTIONS 36-40: Each of the following sentences has a word or phrase underlined. Below each sentence are four other words or phrases. Choose the word or phrase that keeps the meaning of the original sentence. Circle the letter of your answer.

36. He worked steadily.
 A. periodically B. without stopping C. repeatedly D. alone

37. He is going to live there temporarily.
 A. for a long time B. in time C. soon D. for a little while

38. She accepted the invitation <u>eagerly</u>.
    A. with interest   B. with surprise   C. unhappily   D. unexpectedly

39. I don't think he's <u>competent</u> to do the job.
    A. old enough   B. needed   C. able   D. willing

40. That's a <u>unique</u> idea.
    A. funny   B. uncommon   C. impossible   D. enormous

PART 8 (20 points)

QUESTIONS 41-45: Read the passage and answer the questions. Circle the letter of the correct answer.

In 1990, revolution broke out in Katmandu, the capital of Nepal. It was a tense time for Julia Chang Bloch, who had just arrived in the country. As the new U.S. ambassador to Nepal, Bloch was responsible for the safety of the nearly 2000 Americans in the country. She did her job competently, and Nepal's new prime minister, K.P. Bhattarai, later described her as a "very impressive person." Julia Chang Bloch was just 48 years old when she became ambassador to Nepal. For someone who had come to the United States as a refugee, this was a remarkable achievement.

Born in China in 1943, Julia Chang lived with her family in the city of Chang Chih-hsing. Her father, who had studied law in the United States, spoke fluent English. In Chang Chih-hsing, he was the head of the customs office, which was an important government position. When the Communists took over in 1949, however, the Chang family left for Hong Kong. From there they got visas to enter the United States.

Although her father spoke English fluently, Julia Chang had never studied the language. When she entered school in the United States, she could not speak English at all. Her father helped her to learn the language and within a year, she had won a speaking contest—in English. More honors followed. After graduating from the University of California at Berkeley, she worked for the Peace Corps in Southeast Asia. Later, she worked at Harvard's Institute of Politics and the Agency for International Development (AID). By the time she left her job with the Agency for International Development, she had risen to head its Asia and Near East bureau. She had also earned a reputation for being an extremely hard worker. Her reputation for getting a job done, as well as her varied background, made her an excellent candidate for the position as ambassador.

BOOK 1: TEST C

41. The revolution in Nepal started

    A. shortly after Bloch arrived in the country.
    B. just before Bloch arrived in the country.
    C. when Bloch arrived in the country.
    D. because Bloch went there.

42. In the first paragraph, the word *remarkable* probably means

    A. funny
    B. scary
    C. unusual
    D. common

43. The purpose of the second paragraph is to

    A. tell about Bloch's experiences in Nepal.
    B. explain how she became an ambassador.
    C. describe Bloch's education.
    D. tell about Bloch's background.

44. When did Bloch's father study law?

    A. Before he went to the United States.
    B. While he was working at the customs office.
    C. After 1949.
    D. While he was in the United States.

45. Which of these statements is **true** about Julia Chang Bloch's career?

    A. She joined the Peace Corps before graduating from the University of California.
    B. For a time, she was the head of AID's Asia and Near East bureau.
    C. She has always worked for the same organization.
    D. All of her jobs have been in the United States.

NAME: _____ DATE: _____ Book 2
Test A
Units 1-3

PART 1 (10 points)

QUESTIONS 1-5: You are going to hear five sentences. You will hear each sentence two times. Choose the sentence on your test paper that is closest in meaning or identical in meaning. Circle the letter of that sentence.

Listen to the example. You will hear: *John's not present in class today.*
You will read:
- A. The class didn't give John a gift.
- B. Today John has a presentation to do in class.
- C. John is absent from class.
- D. John's not the president of his class.

The correct answer is *C.* Sentence C has the same meaning as the sentence you heard, "John's not present in class today." Now get ready to listen to the five sentences.

1.
   - A. This radio isn't working.
   - B. There is something wrong with this radio.
   - C. There is nothing wrong with this radio.
   - D. This is the wrong radio.

2.
   - A. She gave me a fascinating book.
   - B. I didn't like the book that she gave me.
   - C. I want to give her a fascinating book.
   - D. She was fascinating.

3.
   - A. The school is giving a party for everyone.
   - B. The school is providing everything for the party.
   - C. The party is going to take place at school.
   - D. The school doesn't want to have a party.

4.
   - A. He got the job because he is good with computers.
   - B. He got the job even though he doesn't know anything about computers.
   - C. He doesn't have enough experience to get a job.
   - D. The company won't give him the job because he doesn't know how to use a computer.

5.
   - A. The students canceled the classes because they were sick.
   - B. Many of the students are sick because classes have been canceled.
   - C. Because many students are ill, there will be no classes today.
   - D. If the students were ill, we would have class today.

PART 2 (10 Points)

QUESTIONS 5-10: You will hear five short conversations between two speakers. At the end of each conversation, you will hear a question. Read the answers on your test paper and circle the letter of the best answer. You will hear the conversation and question two times.

Listen to the following example.

You will hear:
      Woman: *Have you been waiting long?*
      Man: *No, I just got here a few minutes ago.*
      Third Voice: *How long has the man been waiting?*

You will read:
      A. For a long time.
      B. For just a few minutes.
      C. A few minutes ago.
      D. In a while.

From the conversation you know that the correct answer is *B*. Now get ready to listen to the five conversations.

6. A. At school.
   B. Since they were children.
   C. When they were children.
   D. For a few days.

7. A. Because she is late.
   B. Because she has to take the test.
   C. Because no one is in the room.
   D. Because she is taking a test.

8. A. She's going to go to class.
   B. She's going to miss class.
   C. She's going to the exhibition.
   D. She's unhappy that she is going to miss it.

9. A. The man went inside to check.
   B. The fire alarm went off.
   C. The man locked the front door.
   D. The man was late.

10. A. The man broke the cup.
    B. Someone broke the cup.
    C. The woman broke the cup.
    D. Someone took the cup.

PART 3 (20 points)

QUESTIONS 11-20: Complete the sentences with the correct tense of the verbs in parentheses. Write your answers on the blank lines.

Dear Madeleine,

Thanks for the phone call. I was getting worried because I (not/hear) _____ from you for so long. My friends Hugh and Silvia
           11
(arrive) _____ tomorrow, so I want to get this letter off to
         12
you today. Silvia (never/be) _____ here, so she will
                              13
probably want to see everything, and we'll spend all week running around the city.

I (survive) _____ my trip to visit Tom last
            14
month. It (be) _____ great fun as you can probably
                15
imagine. Tom now (live) _____ in an incredible house in
                         16
the woods that he (finish) _____ building last year. It
                            17
took him three years to build the house because he (hurt) _____ his back in the middle of the project. Then, he
                  18
(just/finish) _____ putting the roof on when there was a
              19
bad storm and a tree (fall) _____ through it. I hear
                             20
someone knocking on the door downstairs, so I'd better go. I'm enclosing some photographs of the family. I'll write again soon.

My best,

Maura

BOOK 2: TEST A

PART 4 (10 points)

QUESTIONS 21-25: Complete the sentences below with one of these transition words: *however, moreover,* or *for example.* Write your answers on the blank lines.

21. Biosphere II is designed to be completely self-sufficient; _____, the air and water inside the structure will be used over and over again.

22. The Biosphere II crew cannot leave the structure; _____, they can communicate with people outside via telephone and computer.

23. Biosphere II houses a tropical forest and a desert; _____, many different kinds of plants will be grown inside.

24. Everything inside of Biosphere II must be recycled; _____, leftover food will be used as fertilizer.

25. Some people think that Biosphere II is a waste of money; _____, I believe that it will help us to learn more about the Earth's environment.

PART 5 (20 points)

QUESTIONS 26-35: Complete the sentences below with an appropriate tense of the verb in parentheses and either the active or passive voice. Write your answers on the blank lines.

The Braille System of Writing

Louis Braille was only fifteen years old when he (invent) _____
26
a new system of writing made up of raised dots. Since the 1820s, the Braille system (use) _____ by millions of blind people all over the
27
world. Today there (be) _____ even watches and musical
28
scores that (write) _____ in Braille.
29

The Ambulance

If you (be) _____30_____ in a serious accident, you would probably have to go to the hospital in an ambulance. The first ambulance (invent) _____31_____ in 1792 by Napoleon's surgeon. Of course, this ambulance (not/have) _____32_____ an engine; it (pull) _____33_____ by a horse.

Seat Belts

Seat belts have been around for longer than you might realize. In the late 1800's, seat belts (use) _____34_____ in some horse-drawn buggies. And in the 1920s, seat belts (be) _____35_____ already standard equipment in civilian aircraft.

PART 6 (10 points)

QUESTIONS 36-40: Each of the following sentences has a word or phrase underlined. Below each sentence are four other words or phrases. Choose the word or phrase that keeps the meaning of the original sentence. Circle the letter of your answer.

36. Your work has improved immensely.
    A. a little   B. very little   C. somewhat   D. a lot

37. Can these bottles be recycled?
    A. used again   B. transported   C. included   D. duplicated

38. Would you mind making a duplicate of this for me?
    A. structure   B. issue   C. payoff   D. copy

39. A lot of people are boycotting that store.
    A. going to   B. staying away from   C. shopping at   D. talking about

40. Fifty percent of the applicants were admitted to the program.
    A. transported   B. reinstated   C. allowed to enter   D. taken

PART 7 (20 points)

QUESTIONS 40-45: Read the passage and answer the questions. Circle the letter of your answer.

Each year in the United States, roughly 180 million tons of trash are generated. Much of this trash is buried in local landfills at a cost to the town. To cut down on the amount of trash going into landfills, many towns have started recycling programs. In these towns, residents are asked to separate newspapers, glass, aluminum, steel, and plastic from their other trash. These recyclable materials are then taken to a material recovery facility where they are separated, decontaminated, and compressed. From there, the materials are taken to mills that can make them into new products.

Of all the trash that is thrown away, paper products make up the largest part. These paper products include cardboard boxes, newspapers, computer printouts, and tissue products. Some of these paper products can be recycled. Cardboard boxes, for example, can become new boxes. Old newspapers can be used to print the news again or to make boxes for dry cereal.

Aluminum is the most valuable material in a town's trash. A ton of compressed aluminum cans might sell for $1000 compared to roughly $50 for a ton of old cardboard boxes. It is estimated that 54.9 billion aluminum cans (9.65 million tons) are recycled in the United States each year.

Plastics have been a big problem in the recycling program. According to the Environmental Protection Agency, only about one tenth of one percent of all plastic products are recycled. Part of the problem is that there are many kinds of plastic, each made from different materials. These different materials cannot be mixed together successfully. Plastics are also very light, and they take up a lot of space. This makes them expensive to collect and transport. To encourage towns to recycle plastics, some manufacturers are now stamping codes on their products so that recyclers can sort them by the materials used in them. Other companies are now helping towns to pay for plastic recycling programs.

Today roughly 10 percent of the population of the United States is involved in recycling programs. This number is increasing as more towns open recycling centers. And as landfill space becomes increasingly scarce and expensive, more towns will understand that it is cheaper to recycle than to throw away.

41. The second paragraph tells about

    A. one type of material that can be recycled.
    B. collecting recyclables.
    C. the most difficult material to recycle.
    D. the amount of trash that is recycled.

42. This reading passage does **not** explain

    A. what a material recovery facility does.
    B. how many tons of trash are created in the United States in a year.
    C. how many aluminum cans are recycled each year.
    D. how many tons of paper are recycled each year.

43. In the first paragraph, the word *generated* probably means

    A. recycled.
    B. collected.
    C. created.
    D. separated.

44. In the last paragraph, the word *scarce* probably means

    A. difficult to find.
    B. useful.
    C. unimportant.
    D. frightening.

45. The main purpose of this reading passage is to

    A. convince someone to start a recycling program.
    B. show that recycling is not very useful.
    C. tell about recycling in the United States.
    D. explain how a material recovery facility works.

NAME: _____ DATE: _____ Book 2
Test B
Units 4-6

PART 1 (10 points)

QUESTIONS 1-5: You are going to hear five sentences. You will hear each sentence two times. Choose the sentence on your test paper that is closest in meaning or identical in meaning. Circle the letter of that sentence.

Listen to the example. You will hear: *John's not present in class today.*
You will read:
- A. The class didn't give John a gift.
- B. Today John has a presentation to do in class.
- C. John is absent from class.
- D. John's not the president of his class.

The correct answer is *C.* Sentence C has the same meaning as the sentence you heard, "John's not present in class today." Now get ready to listen to the five sentences.

1.
   - A. It is certain that he called while you were out.
   - B. It's possible that he called when you weren't there.
   - C. He was able to call but he didn't.
   - D. He was supposed to call but he didn't have time.

2.
   - A. He wasn't able to come.
   - B. He was supposed to come, but he didn't want to.
   - C. He came even though he didn't want to.
   - D. He was able to come, but he chose not to.

3.
   - A. He was late because he got that phone call.
   - B. He got the phone call because he was late.
   - C. He didn't get the phone call because he was late.
   - D. He would have been late if he had gotten that phone call.

4.
   - A. She stayed up so late that she couldn't finish the book.
   - B. Because it was late, she couldn't finish the book.
   - C. If she had stayed up late, she would have finished the book.
   - D. In order to finish the book, she stayed up late.

5.
   - A. He is too tired to stay awake.
   - B. He is too tired to go to sleep.
   - C. If he were more tired, he would go to sleep.
   - D. He is tired because of his eyes.

PART 2 (10 Points)

QUESTIONS 5-10: You will hear five short conversations between two speakers. At the end of each conversation, you will hear a question. Read the answers on your test paper and circle the letter of the best answer. You will hear the conversation and question two times.

Listen to the following example.

You will hear:

      Woman: *Have you been waiting long?*
      Man: *No, I just got here a few minutes ago.*
      Third Voice: *How long has the man been waiting?*

You will read:
    A. For a long time.
    B. For just a few minutes.
    C. A few minutes ago.
    D. In a while.

From the conversation you know that the correct answer is *B*. Now get ready to listen to the five conversations.

6. A. He didn't go to the party.
    B. He didn't enjoy the party.
    C. He didn't take his camera to the party.
    D. He didn't see his friends at the party.

7. A. She couldn't have called earlier.
    B. She is impossible.
    C. She has been at home all day.
    D. She is getting upset.

8. A. He's going to go to the soccer game and then do his homework.
    B. He's going to play soccer all day.
    C. He's going to help the woman with her homework.
    D. He's going to spend the day doing his homework.

9. A. Because she is sick.
    B. Because she's at home.
    C. Because of school
    D. Because she likes it much better.

10. A. At nine.
     B. Before nine.
     C. After nine.
     D. In the afternoon.

BOOK 2: TEST B

PART 3 (10 points)

QUESTIONS 11-15: Complete the sentences with the correct tense of the verbs in parentheses. Write your answers on the blank lines.

11. Stephanie doesn't have a car. If she (have) _____ a car, she wouldn't have to take the bus to work.

12. Andy didn't go to class yesterday. If he (go) _____ to class, he would have known about the test today.

13. Can you give me a ride home? If you (give) _____ me a ride, I won't have to take a taxi.

14. I forgot to pick you up because you didn't remind me. If you had reminded me,

    I (not/forget) _____ .

15. Jake can hardly keep his eyes open. If he hadn't stayed up so late last night, he

    (not/be) _____ tired now.

PART 4 (20 points)

QUESTIONS 16-25: In each of the following sentences, one of the four underlined parts is wrong. Write the letter of the wrong part in the blank. IMPORTANT: Do not correct the wrong part of the sentence; just write the letter in the blank.

Example: __C__ Last week John got on the bus and went to his sister new
                A   B   C
          apartment to visit her.
                 D

The correct answer is C. The underlined word *sister* is incorrect.

_____ 16. My brother bought a computer last year so that he did his work more
         A   B   C   D
         efficiently.
         E

_____ 17. He gained so many weight while he was on vacation that he had to go on
         A B   C   D
         a strict diet.

_____ 18. If she hadn't spent so much money at the beginning of the trip, she
           A   B C
         wouldn't have run out of money before she gets home.
                         D

_____ 19. They wanted <u>to</u> expand the restaurant so <u>than</u> they <u>could</u> serve <u>more</u>
                        A   B   C   D
people.

_____ 20. Because <u>of</u> the class was <u>cancelled</u>, <u>no one</u> had <u>to get up</u> early.
                          A   B   C   D

_____ 21. Sharon <u>had decided</u> to stay for <u>an</u> extra week <u>because</u> the weather in
                              A   B   C
California <u>is</u> beautiful now.
            D

_____ 22. If you <u>get</u> here <u>later than</u> midnight, <u>everyone</u> will probably <u>been</u> sleeping.
                A   B   C   D

_____ 23. I asked <u>him</u> <u>to get</u> me a video, that he <u>had seen</u> and enjoyed.
              A   B   C   D

_____ 24. If you <u>buy</u> a car in order <u>get</u> to school, how <u>are</u> you going to be able
              A   B   C
<u>to pay</u> for the gasoline?
  D

_____ 25. You should have <u>tell</u> me that you <u>were</u> going to throw out all <u>of</u> the old
                           A   B   C
furniture that <u>was</u> upstairs.
                 D

PART 5 (10 points)

QUESTIONS 26-30: Complete each dialogue with the correct form of the verb in parentheses and the modal *could, should, might,* or *must.* Write your answers on the blank lines.

26. A: Do you know where Alex is?
    B: No, I don't. He (be) _____ in class today but he wasn't.

27. A: What's wrong?
    B: I can't find my wallet. I (left) _____ it at home, but I'm not sure.

28. A: I didn't see you at the party last night. Did you have trouble finding a ride?
    B: No, I (go) _____ with Laura, but I wasn't feeling well.

29. A: This food looks great! Did you bring it?
    B: No, I didn't. Gina or Philip (bring) _____ it, but I'm not sure.

30. A: Who washed the dishes?
    B: It (be) _____ Ellie. She was the only one at home.

BOOK 2: TEST B

PART 6 (10 points)

QUESTIONS 31-35: Rewrite each of the sentences below using the words in parentheses. Write your new sentences on the blank lines.

31. He took a plane so that he would get there faster.
    (in order to) _____

32. It was so noisy that I couldn't hear him.
    (because of) _____

33. Due to problems with the electricity, the library will be closed today.
    (because) _____

34. He called his sister to apologize for missing dinner.
    (so that) _____

35. He got a stomachache because he ate too many apples.
    (so many/much ...that) _____

PART 7 (10 points)

QUESTIONS 36-40: Each of the following sentences has a word or phrase underlined. Below each sentence are four other words or phrases. Choose the word or phrase that keeps the meaning of the original sentence. Circle the letter of your answer.

36. I haven't <u>come up</u> with a solution yet.
    A. looked up   B. heard   C. found   D. received

37. You'll see him if you <u>hurry</u>.
    A. stand up   B. go quickly   C. try   D. walk

38. Using a computer <u>enabled</u> him to do the work quickly.
    A. permitted   B. caused   C. taught   D. made

39. You must be <u>elated</u> by the news!
    A. upset   B. surprised   C. made happy   D. confused

40. It was too late to <u>rescue</u> the animal.
    A. punish   B. feed   C. reward   D. save

PART 8 (20 points)

QUESTIONS 40-45: Read the passage and answer the questions. Circle the letter of your answer.

If you had lived several hundred years ago, you wouldn't have worn shoes. Instead, you would have worn schewis or shooys. Over the years, the English word *shoe* has been spelled in at least seventeen different ways. The earliest Anglo-Saxon word was *sceo* which means *to cover*. This eventually became *schewis* in the plural and later *shooys*. Today, of course, we call them *shoes*. And the spelling of the word *shoes* isn't the only thing that has changed. Shoe styles have gone through some extraordinary transformations, too.

Perhaps one of the most dangerous shoe styles was the fourteenth century English crakow. The crakow was a shoe with a very long toe. Every year the tip of this popular shoe got a little bit longer. In fact, the crakow got so long that King Edward III finally enacted a law prohibiting shoes that extended more than two inches beyond the human toe. The law must not have been popular. By the early 1400s, people could be seen wearing shoes with tips of eighteen inches. They could also be seen routinely tripping over the ends of their very long shoes.

In the 1500s, a German shoe called the pump became popular in Europe. This shoe was a type of loose slipper with a low heel. Its name may have come from the sound that the shoe made on a wooden floor—plump, plump, plump.

High-heeled shoes were popular in sixteenth-century France. Unlike today, however, these shoes were first worn by men. The King of France, Louis XIV, may have started this fad. Because he was short, he added a few inches to the heels of his shoes so that he would appear taller. Eager to be in style, the men and women at court hurried to copy him. This, of course, forced the King to increase the height of his own shoes.

If high heels and pointed toes are popular today, you can almost be certain that they won't be popular tomorrow. Shoe styles seem to change faster than you can wear out your old shoes. Who knows what will be in style tomorrow. Let's just hope that it is not the crakow.

41. What is the main topic of this passage?

    A. How the spelling of the word *shoes* has changed.
    B. How shoe styles have changed.
    C. Why the crakow was dangerous.
    D. What people wore in the past.

42. In the first paragraph, the word *transformations* probably means

    A. spellings.
    B. ways.
    C. uses.
    D. changes.

43. Which statement is true according to the reading passage?

    A. The crakow was an unpopular type of shoe.
    B. People stopped wearing the crakow because of King Edward's law.
    C. The crakow got longer after King Edward enacted his law.
    D. The crakow was popular in the 1600s.

44. From the reading, which statement is true about the pump?

    A. It didn't have a high heel.
    B. It was similar to the crakow.
    C. It was not very comfortable.
    D. It was popular for many years.

45. Which of the following questions is **not** answered in the passage?

    A. When were high-heeled shoes popular in France?
    B. How did the pump get its name?
    C. Why did people stop wearing the crakow?
    D. Why did Louis XIV wear high-heeled shoes?

NAME: _____ DATE: _____   Book 2
                                                     Test C
                                                     Units 7-9

PART 1 (10 points)

QUESTIONS 1-5: You are going to hear five sentences. You will hear each sentence two times. Choose the sentence on your test paper that is closest in meaning or identical in meaning. Circle the letter of that sentence.

Listen to the example. You will hear: *John's not present in class today.*
You will read:
   A. The class didn't give John a gift.
   B. Today John has a presentation to do in class.
   C. John is absent from class.
   D. John's not the president of his class.

The correct answer is *C*. Sentence C has the same meaning as the sentence you heard, "John's not present in class today." Now get ready to listen to the five sentences.

1. A. She said, "I didn't go to the movies."
   B. She said, "I'm going to go to the movies."
   C. She said, "I'm not going to go to the movies."
   D. She said, "I can't go to the movies."

2. A. "Don't wait for me," he said to his daughter.
   B. "Wait for me," he said to his daughter.
   C. "Don't write to me," he said to his daughter.
   D. "Don't wait for your sister," he said to his daughter.

3. A. "Are you going to eat lunch?" she asked.
   B. "When did you eat lunch?" she asked.
   C. "Did you make lunch?" she asked.
   D. "Did you eat lunch?" she asked.

4. A. I'm sorry that I took that course.
   B. I'm sorry that I didn't take that course.
   C. I hope to take that course.
   D. I'm glad I didn't take that course.

5. A. I will finish my work when you get here.
   B. After you get here, I will finish my work.
   C. If you get here, I will finish my work.
   D. My work will be done before you get here.

BOOK 2: TEST C

PART 2 (10 Points)

QUESTIONS 5-10: You will hear five short conversations between two speakers. At the end of each conversation, you will hear a question. Read the answers on your test paper and circle the letter of the best answer. You will hear the conversation and question two times.

Listen to the following example.

You will hear:

        Woman: *Have you been waiting long?*
        Man: *No, I just got here a few minutes ago.*
        Third Voice: *How long has the man been waiting?*

You will read:
- A. For a long time.
- B. For just a few minutes.
- C. A few minutes ago.
- D. In a while.

From the conversation you know that the correct answer is *B*. Now get ready to listen to the five conversations.

6.
   - A. She asked him where he was going.
   - B. She said if he was going to the library.
   - C. She asked when he was going.
   - D. She asked him about the library.

7.
   - A. In the library
   - B. In class
   - C. In a car
   - D. In a plane

8.
   - A. She wanted to know how to get there.
   - B. She wanted to know how Peter had gotten there.
   - C. She wanted to know how the man had gotten there.
   - D. She wanted to get to know Peter.

9.
   - A. He has to take a test.
   - B. He has to take the test again.
   - C. He is looking forward to the test.
   - D. He is wishing the test were over.

10.
    - A. He said he was living there.
    - B. He said he wasn't going to leave.
    - C. He said he didn't know.
    - D. He said he was going to leave soon.

PART 3 (20 points)

Read each short conversation. Use the information in the conversations to complete the sentences. Use indirect speech. Write your answers on the blank lines.

Example: Sandra: When will you get to New York?
Leila: I probably won't get there until noon.

Sandra asked Leila _when she would get to New York._
Leila said _that she probably wouldn't get there until noon._

Ted: Did you have any trouble finding it?
Jon: No, I didn't.

11. Ted asked Jon _____
12. Jon said _____

Tania: Where's the car?
Alex: I parked it in back.

13. Tania asked Alex _____
14. Alex said _____

Stacey: When did Jack leave?
Marilyn: Before nine.

15. Stacey asked Marilyn _____
16. Marilyn said _____

Kip: Is Tab inside?
Sarah: No, he isn't.

17. Kip asked _____
18. Sarah said _____

Peter: Do you know where Anne went?
Josh: I think she went to the store.

19. Peter asked Josh _____
20. Josh said _____

BOOK 2: TEST C

PART 4 (20 points)

In each of the following sentences, one of the four underlined parts is wrong. Write the letter of the wrong part in the blank. IMPORTANT: Do not correct the wrong part of the sentence; just write the letter of your answer in the blank.

Example: __C__   Last week John <u>got</u> on the bus and went to his <u>sister</u> new
       A   B   C

        apartment to visit <u>her</u>.
               D

  The correct answer is *C*. The underlined word *sister* is wrong.

_____ 21. If you <u>are</u> interested <u>to go</u> to the beach, I'm planning <u>to drive</u> there
       A   B   C

   as soon as I <u>have finished</u> my work.
         D

_____ 22. I hope <u>to take</u> a trip <u>at</u> the end of the month, but I'm not sure that I
      A   B   C

   <u>would</u> have enough money.
    D

_____ 23. Since I <u>got</u> this computer, I <u>haven't had</u> much time to use <u>them</u>, but I
       A   B   C

   hope to have <u>more</u> time next month.
         D

_____ 24. I wish I <u>had know</u> that you <u>were thinking</u> of <u>buying</u> a house <u>that</u> is so
       A   B   C   D

   far away.

_____ 25. I was very surprised <u>when</u> Marla asked <u>that</u> I <u>wanted</u> <u>to borrow</u> her new
           A   B   C   D

   car.

_____ 26. By next year, we <u>will have</u> finished building <u>our</u> new house and <u>pay</u>
         A   B   C

   for <u>it</u>.
    D

_____ 27. I wish that you <u>will</u> spend some time <u>looking</u> for a job <u>that</u> uses <u>your</u>
        A   B   C   D

   skills.

_____ 28. If you had told me that <u>your's</u> car <u>was</u> for sale, I <u>might have</u> bought <u>it</u>.
          A   B   C   D

_____ 29. <u>Can</u> you <u>told</u> me what time the bus <u>is</u> supposed <u>to get</u> here?
         A   B   C   D

_____ 30. She told me <u>to call</u> Mr. Martin, <u>which</u> is the president of the company,
                    A   B

because he <u>is</u> in charge of <u>hiring</u>.
         C   D

PART 5 (10 points)

Read each of the short conversations below. Use the information in the conversation to answer the question that follows. Write your answer on the blank line.

31. Alicia: Where's Jake?

    Tom: I have no idea.

    Tom doesn't know _____

32. Carlos: Why aren't the lights working?

    Yan: I don't know.

    Yan can't explain _____

33. Mei: Why did Sergio get angry?

    Kay: I don't know. I didn't ask him.

    Kay didn't ask Sergio _____

34. Mike: How long is this movie.

    Kitty: I have no idea.

    Kitty has no idea _____

35. Jaime: Can you tell me where the post office is?

    Ted: I'm sorry. I'm new in town too.

    Ted and Jaime don't know _____

PART 6 (10 points)

Each of the following sentences has a word or phrase underlined. Below each sentence are four other words or phrases. Circle the letter of the word or phrase that keeps the meaning of the original sentence.

36. Your story intrigues me.
    A. shocks   B. bores   C. confuses   D. interests

37. It was a crucial decision.
    A. very important   B. difficult   C. unpopular   D. special

38. His looks have changed considerably.
    A. unnecessarily   B. thoughtlessly   C. probably   D. a lot

39. I need to go over this.
    A. look again at   B. replace   C. renovate   D. remove

40. I can't figure this out.
    A. use this   B. understand this   C. draw this   D. measure this

PART 7 (20 points)

Read the passage and answer the questions. Circle the letter of your answer.

Hank Van Buren had worked for a major accounting firm for almost fifteen years when the company was sold. "When the company changed hands, many employees got laid off or moved around the company. I had the choice of changing jobs within the company or leaving the company altogether. I decided it was time to leave," Van Buren said.

Instead of looking for a job with another large company, Mr. Van Buren decided to go out on his own—or almost on his own. Van Buren decided to start his own business, but with some help. He bought a Charter Business Services franchise for $25,000 and set up an office in his home. With the franchise's network of accountants to help when he had a problem, Van Buren would provide tax, accounting, and consulting services to small businesses.

"I didn't like it at first," Mr. Van Buren said. "I was used to working with a lot of people. Suddenly I was all by myself working out of a bedroom in my house." Van Buren's business did well, however, and before long he had moved into an office outside of his home and hired another accountant.

For many people, buying a franchise is the only viable way to get into business. According to Mr. Van Buren, buying a franchise gives you a much better chance of success than starting up your own business. According to the Small Business Administration, independent business start-ups have a failure rate of 80 percent. Statistics for franchises, however, indicate a failure rate of no more than 5 percent. For Mr. Van Buren, buying a franchise allowed him to operate under the name of a well-known company. While he had to follow the rules and regulations of the company, he got help in organizing and managing the franchise. When he had problems, he could turn to the company for help. Buying a franchise might not be right for everyone, but for Mr. Van Buren, it was the best choice.

41. The first paragraph explains

    A. how Mr. Van Buren learned about franchises.
    B. why Mr. Van Buren left the accounting firm.
    C. what Mr. Van Buren did after he left the company.
    D. what services a franchise provides.

42. In the reading passage, Mr. Van Buren said that

    A. he didn't like working with a lot of people.
    B. he wished he had stayed with the company.
    C. in the beginning it wasn't easy to work at home.
    D. he hoped to work alone in the future.

43. Which of the following statements is **not** true according to the passage?

    A. Eighty percent of all franchises fail.
    B. A franchise owner must follow the rules of the company.
    C. Mr. Van Buren had experience in accounting before he bought a franchise.
    D. A franchise owner gets help from the company.

44. In the fourth paragraph, the word *viable* probably means

    A. useless.
    B. practical.
    C. foolish.
    D. expensive.

45. The reading passage did **not** explain

    A. why Mr. Van Buren left the the accounting firm.
    B. how much Mr. Van Buren paid for the franchise.
    C. what the advantages of buying a franchise are.
    D. where Mr. Van Buren learned about franchises.

PERSPECTIVES 2000 TESTS

Scripts and Answer Keys

BOOK 1: TEST A
Script

PART 1 (10 points)

QUESTIONS 1-5: You will hear five short conversations between two speakers. At the end of each conversation, you will hear a question. Read the answers on your test paper and circle the letter of the best answer. You will hear the conversation and question two times.

Listen to the following example.

You will hear:
    Woman: Have you been waiting long?
    Man: No, I just got here a few minutes ago.
    Third Voice: How long has the man been waiting for the woman?

    Woman: Have you been waiting long?
    Man: No, I just got here a few minutes ago.
    Third Voice: How long has the man been waiting for the woman?

You will read:
    A. For a long time.
    B. For just a few minutes.
    C. A few minutes ago.
    D. In a while.

From the conversation you know that the correct answer is (B) for just a few minutes. Now get ready to listen to the five conversations.

Number One.
    Woman: I'm ready to leave whenever you are.
    Man: Okay. Let's go.
    Third voice: When are the man and woman planning to leave?

Number One.
    Woman: I'm ready to leave whenever you are.
    Man: Okay. Let's go.
    Third voice: When are the man and woman planning to leave?

<pause 12 seconds>

Number Two.
    Man: Why don't you call them?
    Woman: I don't think they'll be at home now.
    Third voice: What does the man want the woman to do?

Number Two.
    Man: Why don't you call them?
    Woman: I don't think they'll be at home now.
    Third voice: What does the man want the woman to do?

<pause 12 seconds>

Number Three.
    Man: Have you filled out the questionnaire yet?
    Woman: No, I haven't, but I'll get it done tonight.
    Third voice: What hasn't the woman done yet?

Number Three.
    Man: Have you filled out the questionnaire yet?
    Woman: No, I haven't, but I'll get it done tonight.
    Third voice: What hasn't the woman done yet?

<pause 12 seconds>

Number Four.
    Woman: Are you getting tired of listening to this music?
    Man: No, not yet.
    Third voice: What are they doing now?

Number Four.
    Woman: Are you getting tired of listening to this music?
    Man: No, not yet.
    Third voice: What are they doing now?

<pause 12 seconds>

Number Five.
    Woman: Did you invite Mark for dinner?
    Man: Oh no, I forgot.
    Third voice: What did the man forget to do?

Number Five.
    Woman: Did you invite Mark for dinner?
    Man: Oh no, I forgot.
    Third voice: What did the man forget to do?

BOOK 1: TEST A
Answer Key

Part 1
1. A
2. C
3. D
4. B
5. C

Part 2
6. answering
7. get up
8. get
9. taking
10. go
11. was watching
12. haven't eaten/didn't eat
13. was walking
14. have known
15. is sleeping

Part 3
16. is ringing
17. didn't have
18. is
19. changes
20. was
21. haven't moved
22. living
23. to go
24. will see/am going to see
25. to see

Part 4
36. C
37. A
38. D
39. D
40. B

Part 5
26. got
27. to stay
28. are
29. ended
30. have been looking
31. have
32. happier
33. feel
34. to write
35. to living

Part 6
41. A
42. C
43. B
44. C
45. A

Note: This passage is adapted from Bureau of the Census Document D-3800-Q

BOOK 1: TEST B
Script

Part 1

QUESTIONS 1-5: You are going to hear five sentences. You will hear each sentence two times. Choose the sentence on your test paper that is closest in meaning or identical in meaning. Circle the letter of that sentence.

Listen to the example.

You will hear: John's not present in class today.
                 John's not present in class today.

You will read:
  A. The class didn't give John a gift.
  B. Today John has a presentation to do in class.
  C. John is absent from class.
  D. John's not the president of his class.

The correct answer is *C*. Sentence C has the same meaning as the sentence you heard, "John's not present in class today." Now get ready to listen to the five sentences.

Number One. He didn't have the right qualifications to get the job.
Number One. He didn't have the right qualifications to get the job.

<pause 12 seconds>

Number Two. In order to graduate, you must pass this course.
Number Two. In order to graduate, you must pass this course.

<pause 12 seconds>

Number Three. If I knew her name, I would tell you.
Number Three. If I knew her name, I would tell you.

<pause 12 seconds>

Number Four. You are not supposed to do that.
Number Four. You are not supposed to do that.

<pause 12 seconds>

Number Five. I might be late because I have to stop at the store.
Number Five. I might be late because I have to stop at the store.

Part 2

QUESTIONS 6-10: You will hear five short conversations between two speakers. At the end of each conversation, you will hear a question. Read the answers on your test paper and circle the letter of the best answer. You will hear the conversation and question two times

Listen to the following example.

You will hear:

    Woman: Have you been waiting long?
    Man: No, I just got here a few minutes ago.
    Third Voice: How long has the man been waiting?

    Woman: Have you been waiting long?
    Man: No, I just got here a few minutes ago.
    Third Voice: How long has the man been waiting?

You will read:
      A. For a long time.
      B. For just a few minutes.
      C. A few minutes ago.
      D. In a while.

From the conversation you know that the correct answer is *B*. Now get ready to listen to the five conversations.

Number Six.
    Woman: I think I'd better leave soon. It's getting late.
    Man: Oh, come on. It's still early. If you leave now, everyone else will leave too.
    Third voice: Where might the two people be?

Number Six.
    Woman: I think I'd better leave soon. It's getting late.
    Man: Oh, come on. It's still early. If you leave now, everyone else will leave too.
    Third voice: Where might the two people be?

<pause 12 seconds>

Number Seven.
    Man: We're having a test tomorrow in English. If I don't study tonight, I'm not going to do very well on it.
    Woman: A test? Tomorrow? I thought we were supposed to have a test on Friday.
    Third voice: What had the man better do?

Number Seven.
    Man: We're having a test tomorrow in English. If I don't study tonight, I'm not going to do very well on it.
    Woman: A test? Tomorrow? I thought we were supposed to have a test on Friday.
    Third voice: What had the man better do?

<pause 12 seconds>

Number Eight.
    Man: What am I supposed to do?
    Woman: Wait here by the phone. Jim will call soon.
    Third Voice: What is the man supposed to do?

Number Eight.
    Man: What am I supposed to do?
    Woman: Wait here by the phone. Jim will call soon.
    Third Voice: What is the man supposed to do?

<pause 12 seconds>

Number Nine.
    Man: If you were I, what would you do?
    Woman: I guess I would take the job. If you don't like it, you can always quit.
    Third Voice: What does the man want advice about?

Number Nine.
    Man: If you were I, what would you do?
    Woman: I guess I would take the job. If you don't like it, you can always quit.
    Third Voice: What does the man want advice about?

<pause 12 seconds>

Number Ten.
    Woman: This book is getting better and better.
    Man: I thought you didn't like it.
    Woman: I didn't like it at first, but now it's pretty good.
    Third Voice: What's the woman's opinion of the book?

Number Ten.
    Woman: This book is getting better and better.
    Man: I thought you didn't like it.
    Woman: I didn't like it at first, but now it's pretty good.
    Third Voice: What's the woman's opinion of the book?

BOOK 1: TEST B
Answer Key

Part 1
1. C
2. B
3. D
4. C
5. A

Part 2
6. B
7. C
8. D
9. A
10. C

Part 3
11. must
12. don't have to
13. must not
14. don't have to
15. don't have to

Part 4
16. B
17. C
18. D
19. C
20. B

Part 5
21. must not
22. must not
23. don't have to
24. have to
25. have to

Part 6
26. must
27. should
28. must
29. should/must
30. might

Part 7
31. studied, would get
32. rains, will take
33. weren't (working), would hear
34. weren't, would/could mail
35. had, would/could get

Part 8
36. D
37. B
38. A
39. C
40. A

Part 9
41. B
42. D
43. B
44. B
45. C

BOOK 1: TEST C
Script

QUESTIONS 1-10: You are going to hear ten short conversations between two speakers. At the end of each conversation, you will hear a statement. Use the information in the conversation to decide if the statement is true or false. Circle TRUE or FALSE. You will hear the conversation and statement two times.

Listen to the following example.

You will hear:
Woman:	I found the book that you lost.
Man:	Great. Where was it?
Woman:	In my car.
Third Voice:	True or False? The woman found the man's book.

Woman:	I found the book that you lost.
Man:	Great. Where was it?
Woman:	In my car.
Third Voice:	True or False? The woman found the man's book.

From the conversation you know that the correct answer is *True*. Now get ready to listen to the conversations.

Number One.
Man:	I want you to meet someone who knows Rita's brother.
Woman:	Really? What's his name?
Man:	Roger.
Third Voice:	True or False. Roger is Rita's brother.

Number One.
Man:	I want you to meet someone who knows Rita's brother.
Woman:	Really? What's his name?
Man:	Roger.
Third Voice:	True or False. Roger is Rita's brother.

<pause 12 seconds>

Number Two.
Woman:	Their restaurant went out of business soon after they opened it.
Man:	Why was that?
Woman:	They didn't advertise enough.
Third Voice:	True or False. The restaurant went out of business because the owners hadn't advertised enough.

Number Two.
Woman:	Their restaurant went out of business soon after they opened it.
Man:	Why was that?
Woman:	They didn't advertise enough.
Third Voice:	True or False. The restaurant went out of business because the owners hadn't advertised enough.

<pause 12 seconds>

Number Three.
- Man: I called last night but no one was home.
- Woman: What time did you call?
- Man: Around 8.
- Woman: Oh. I didn't get home until 9.
- Third Voice: True or False. When the man called, the woman hadn't gotten home yet.

Number Three.
- Man: I called last night but no one was home.
- Woman: What time did you call?
- Man: Around 8.
- Woman: Oh. I didn't get home until 9.
- Third Voice: True or False. When the man called, the woman hadn't gotten home yet.

<pause 12 seconds>

Number Four.
- Woman: I was getting worried. What happened?
- Man: Sorry I'm late. There was a lot of traffic. Let's get going. If the car doesn't break down, we'll still get there in time.
- Third Voice: True or False. The man was late because his car had broken down.

Number Four.
- Woman: I was getting worried. What happened?
- Man: Sorry I'm late. There was a lot of traffic. Let's get going. If the car doesn't break down, we'll still get there in time.
- Third Voice: True or False. The man was late because his car had broken down.

<pause 12 seconds>

Number Five.
- Young man: Ma, can I borrow the car?
- Woman: I guess so. But please drive carefully.
- Third Voice: True or False. The woman is going to let her son use the car.

Number Five.
- Young man: Ma, can I borrow the car?
- Woman: I guess so. But please drive carefully.
- Third Voice: True or False. The woman is going to let her son use the car.

<pause 12 seconds>

Number Six.
- Man: I'm a little angry with Jim.
- Woman: What's the problem?
- Man: I asked him to clean up his room, but he didn't do it.
- Third Voice: True or False. The man got Jim to clean up his room.

Number Six.
- Man: I'm a little angry with Jim.
- Woman: What's the problem?
- Man: I asked him to clean up his room, but he didn't do it.
- Third Voice: True or False. The man got Jim to clean up his room.

<pause 12 seconds>

Number Seven.
- Woman: Did anyone take the book that I left on kitchen table?
- Man: I haven't seen it.
- Woman: I'm sure I put it there.
- Third Voice: True or False. The man took the book that the woman had left on the kitchen table.

Number Seven.
- Woman: Did anyone take the book that I left on kitchen table?
- Man: I haven't seen it.
- Woman: I'm sure I put it there.
- Third Voice: True or False. The man took the book that the woman had left on the kitchen table.

<pause 12 seconds>

Number Eight.
- Man: I hear that Taka has a new job.
- Woman: Yeah. She's working for a company in San Diego. It does environmental studies.
- Man: Really? That sounds interesting.
- Third Voice: True or False. Taka works for a company that does environmental studies.

Number Eight.
- Man: I hear that Taka has a new job.
- Woman: Yeah. She's working for a company in San Diego. It does environmental studies.
- Man: Really? That sounds interesting.
- Third Voice: True or False. Taka works for a company that does environmental studies.

<pause 12 seconds>

Number Nine.
- Woman: It sure is raining hard. Did you get wet?
- Man: No, I got here before it started to rain.
- Third Voice: True or False. It had already started to rain by the time the man arrived.

Number Nine.
- Woman: It sure is raining hard. Did you get wet?
- Man: No, I got here before it started to rain.
- Third Voice: True or False. It had already started to rain by the time the man arrived.

<pause 12 seconds>

Number Ten.
    Man: Were you able to get Sam to fix the car.
    Woman: He was eager to do it. Can you believe it?
    Third Voice: True or False. Sam refused to fix the car.

Number Ten.
    Man: Were you able to get Sam to fix the car.
    Woman: He was eager to do it. Can you believe it?
    Third Voice: True or False. Sam refused to fix the car.

BOOK 1: TEST C
Answer Key

Part 1
1. False
2. True
3. True
4. False
5. True
6. False
7. False
8. True
9. False
10. False

Part 2
11. Ken has been working/has worked at DECA since 1990.
12. When Ken got a job at IBC, he had just graduated from college.
13. Ken worked for IBC for ten years.
14. Since he left IBC, Ken has worked/has been working at DECA.
15. In 1979, Ken hadn't graduated from college yet.

Part 3
16. C
17. E
18. B
19. D
20. A

Part 4
21. to come
22. do
23. go
24. to move
25. do

Part 5
Sample answers.
26. On my way home, I met someone who looks just like you.
27. On my way to school, I talked to someone whom you know.
28. The letter that I sent took three weeks to go from California to Florida.
29. The woman whose house burned down has moved away.
30. The area in which they live is unique.

Part 6	Part 7	Part 8
31. D	36. B	41. A
32. A	37. D	42. C
33. A	38. A	43. D
34. A	39. C	44. D
35. A	40. B	45. B

BOOK 2: TEST A
Script

PART 1 (10 points)

QUESTIONS 1-5: You are going to hear five sentences. You will hear each sentence two times. Choose the sentence on your test paper that is closest in meaning or identical in meaning. Circle the letter of that sentence.

    Listen to the example.
    You will hear: John's not present in class today.
                              John's not present in class today.

    You will read:
           A. The class didn't give John a gift.
           B. Today John has a presentation to do in class.
           C. John is absent from class.
           D. John's not the president of his class.

The correct answer is *C*. Sentence C has the same meaning as the sentence you heard, "John's not present in class today." Now get ready to listen to the five sentences.

Number One.	There isn't anything wrong with this radio.
Number One.	There isn't anything wrong with this radio.

<pause 12 seconds>

Number Two.	The book that she gave me was fascinating.
Number Two.	The book that she gave me was fascinating.

<pause 12 seconds>

Number Three.	Everything for the party is being provided by the school.
Number Three.	Everything for the party is being provided by the school.

<pause 12 seconds>

Number Four.	If he knew something about computers, the company would give him the job.
Number Four.	If he knew something about computers, the company would give him the job.

<pause 12 seconds>

Number Five.   Classes have been canceled for today because many of the students are sick.
Number Five.   Classes have been canceled for today because many of the students are sick.

PART 2

QUESTIONS 6-10: You will hear five short conversations between two speakers. At the end of each conversation, you will hear a question. Read the answers on your test paper and circle the letter of the best answer. You will hear the conversation and question two times.

Listen to the following example.

You will hear:
- Woman: Have you been waiting long?
- Man: No, I just got here a few minutes ago.
- Third Voice: How long has the man been waiting?

- Woman: Have you been waiting long?
- Man: No, I just got here a few minutes ago.
- Third Voice: How long has the man been waiting?

You will read:
- A. For a long time.
- B. For just a few minutes.
- C. A few minutes ago.
- D. In a while.

From the conversation you know that the correct answer is *B*. Now get ready to listen to the five conversations.

Number Six.
- Man: How long have you known José?
- Woman: For a long time. We went to school together when we were children.
- Third Voice: How long has the woman known José?

Number Six.
- Man: How long have you known José?
- Woman: For a long time. We went to school together when we were children.
- Third Voice: How long has the woman known José?

<pause 12 seconds>

Number Seven.
- Man: I'm sorry but no one is allowed to enter this room. A test is being given.
- Woman: I know. I'm supposed to be taking the test.
- Man: I'm sorry but the test has already started.
- Third Voice: Why can't the woman go into the room?

Number Seven.
- Man: I'm sorry but no one is allowed to enter this room. A test is being given.
- Woman: I know. I'm supposed to be taking the test.
- Man: I'm sorry but the test has already started.
- Third Voice: Why can't the woman go into the room?

<pause 12 seconds>

Number Eight.
- Man: Are you going to the exhibition tonight?
- Woman: Unfortunately, I'm going to miss it. If I didn't have a class, I would go.
- Third Voice: What is the woman going to do tonight?

Number Eight.
- Man: Are you going to the exhibition tonight?
- Woman: Unfortunately, I'm going to miss it. If I didn't have a class, I would go.
- Third Voice: What is the woman going to do tonight?

<pause 12 seconds>

Number Nine.
- Man: Sorry I'm late. I had just locked the front door when the fire alarm went off.
- Woman: Was something on fire?
- Man: No, but I had to go back inside to check carefully.
- Third Voice: What happened first?

Number Nine.
- Man: Sorry I'm late. I had just locked the front door when the fire alarm went off.
- Woman: Was something on fire?
- Man: No, but I had to go back inside to check carefully.
- Third Voice: What happened first?

<pause 12 seconds>

Number Ten.
- Man: How did this cup get broken?
- Woman: I don't know. It was broken when I got here.
- Third Voice: What happened to the cup?

Number Ten.
Man: How did this cup get broken?
Woman: I don't know. It was broken when I got here.
Third Voice: What happened to the cup?

BOOK 2: TEST A
Answer Key

Part 1
1. C
2. A
3. B
4. D
5. C

Part 2
6. B
7. A
8. A
9. C
10. B

Part 3
11. hadn't heard
12. will arrive/are going to arrive/are arriving
13. has never been
14. survived
15. was
16. lives/is living
17. finished
18. hurt
19. had just finished
20. fell

Part 4
21. for example
22. however
23. moreover
24. for example
25. however

Part 5
26. invented
27. has been used
28. are
29. are written
30. were
31. was invented
32. didn't have/did not have
33. was pulled
34. were used
35. were

Part 6
36. D
37. A
38. D
39. B
40. C

Part 7
41. A
42. D
43. C
44. A
45. C

BOOK 2: TEST B
Script

PART 1 (10 points)

QUESTIONS 1-5: You are going to hear five sentences. You will hear each sentence two times. Choose the sentence on your test paper that is closest in meaning or identical in meaning. Circle the letter of that sentence.

Listen to the example.
You will hear: John's not present in class today.
John's not present in class today.

You will read:
A. The class didn't give John a gift.
B. Today John has a presentation to do in class.
C. John is absent from class.
D. John's not the president of his class.

The correct answer is *C*. Sentence C has the same meaning as the sentence you heard, "John's not present in class today." Now get ready to listen to the five sentences.

Number One.   He might have called when you were out.
Number One.   He might have called when you were out.

<pause 12 seconds>

Number Two.   He could have come, but he didn't want to.
Number Two.   He could have come, but he didn't want to.

<pause 12 seconds>

Number Three.   If he hadn't gotten that phone call, he wouldn't have been late.
Number Three.   If he hadn't gotten that phone call, he wouldn't have been late.

<pause 12 seconds>

Number Four.   She stayed up late because she wanted to finish the book.
Number Four.   She stayed up late because she wanted to finish the book.

<pause 12 seconds>

Number Five.   He is so tired that he can't keep his eyes open.
Number Five.   He is so tired that he can't keep his eyes open.

PART 2

QUESTIONS 5-10: You will hear five short conversations between two speakers. At the end of each conversation, you will hear a question. Read the answers on your test paper and circle the letter of the best answer. You will hear the conversation and question two times.

Listen to the following example:

You will hear:

    Woman: Have you been waiting long?
    Man: No, I just got here a few minutes ago.
    Third Voice: How long has the man been waiting?

    Woman: Have you been waiting long?
    Man: No, I just got here a few minutes ago.
    Third Voice: How long has the man been waiting?

You will read:
    A. For a long time.
    B. For just a few minutes.
    C. A few minutes ago.
    D. In a while.

From the conversation you know that the correct answer is *B*. Now get ready to listen to the five conversations.

Number Six.
    Woman: How was the party?
    Man: It was great, but I should have taken my camera. All my old friends were there.
    Third Voice: What didn't the man do?

Number Six.
    Woman: How was the party?
    Man: It was great, but I should have taken my camera. All my old friends were there.
    Third Voice: What didn't the man do?

<pause 12 seconds>

Number Seven.
    Man: I wonder why Silvia is late.
    Woman: Don't get upset. She probably tried to call earlier.
    Man: That's impossible. I've been here all day and the phone hasn't rung once.
    Third Voice: What does the man know about Silvia?

Number Seven.
    Man: I wonder why Silvia is late.
    Woman: Don't get upset. She probably tried to call earlier.
    Man: That's impossible. I've been here all day and the phone hasn't rung once.
    Third Voice: What does the man know about Silvia?

<pause 12 seconds>

Number Eight.
    Woman: Are you going to the soccer game?
    Man: I can't. I've got so much homework to do that it will take all day to finish it.
    Third Voice: What is the man going to do today?

Number Eight.
    Woman: Are you going to the soccer game?
    Man: I can't. I've got so much homework to do that it will take all day to finish it.
    Third Voice: What is the man going to do today?

<pause 12 seconds>

Number Nine.
    Man: Did you see Paula today?
    Woman: Yes, I stopped by her house after school. She feels much better, but she's still not ready to go back to work.
    Third Voice: Why isn't Paula going to work?

Number Nine.
    Man: Did you see Paula today?
    Woman: Yes, I stopped by her house after school. She feels much better, but she's still not ready to go back to work.
    Third Voice: Why isn't Paula going to work?

<pause 12 seconds>

Number Ten.
    Woman: How soon do you have to leave?
    Man: Well, if I leave the house a little before nine, I should get there on time.
    Woman: Are you sure that gives you enough time?
    Man: Yes, that should give me plenty of time.
    Third Voice: When will the man be leaving the house?

Number Ten.
    Woman: How soon do you have to leave?
    Man: Well, if I leave the house a little before nine, I should get there on time.
    Woman: Are you sure that gives you enough time?
    Man: Yes, that should give me plenty of time.
    Third Voice: When will the man be leaving the house?

BOOK 2: TEST B
Answer Key

Part 1
    1. B
    2. D
    3. A
    4. D
    5. A

Part 2
    6. C
    7. A
    8. D
    9. A
    10. B

Part 3
    11. had
    12. had gone
    13. give/can give
    14. wouldn't have forgotten
    15. wouldn't be

Part 4
    16. C
    17. B
    18. D
    19. B
    20. A
    21. A
    22. D
    23. C
    24. B
    25. A

Part 5
26. should have been
27. might have left/could have left
28. could have gone
29. might have brought/could have brought
30. must have been

Part 6
31. He took a plane in order to get there faster.
32. I couldn't hear him because of the noise.
33. The library will be closed today because there are problems with the electricity.
    Because of problems with the electricity, the library will be closed today.
34. He called his sister so that he could apologize for missing dinner.
35. He ate so many apples that he got a stomachache.

Part 7
36. C
37. B
38. A
39. C
40. D

Part 8
41. B
42. D
43. C
44. A
45. C

BOOK 2: TEST C
Script

Part 1

QUESTIONS 1-5: You are going to hear five sentences. You will hear each sentence two times. Choose the sentence on your test paper that is closest in meaning or identical in meaning. Circle the letter of that sentence.

Listen to the example.
You will hear: John's not present in class today.
John's not present in class today.

You will read:
A. The class didn't give John a gift.
B. Today John has a presentation to do in class.
C. John is absent from class.
D. John's not the president of his class.

The correct answer is *C*. Sentence C has the same meaning as the sentence you heard, "John's not present in class today." Now get ready to listen to the five sentences.

Number One. She said that she wasn't going to go to the movies.
Number One. She said that she wasn't going to go to the movies.

<pause 12 seconds>

59

Number Two. He told his daughter not to wait for him.
Number Two. He told his daughter not to wait for him.

<pause 12 seconds>

Number Three. She asked if he had eaten lunch.
Number Three. She asked if he had eaten lunch.

<pause 12 seconds>

Number Four. I wish that I had taken that course.
Number Four. I wish that I had taken that course.

<pause 12 seconds>

Number Five. By the time you get here, I will have finished my work.
Number Five. By the time you get here, I will have finished my work.

PART 2

QUESTIONS 5-10: You will hear five short conversations between two speakers. At the end of each conversation, you will hear a question. Read the answers on your test paper and circle the letter of the best answer. You will hear the conversation and question two times.

Listen to the following example:

You will hear:
    Woman: Have you been waiting long?
    Man: No, I just got here a few minutes ago.
    Third Voice: How long has the man been waiting?

    Woman: Have you been waiting long?
    Man: No, I just got here a few minutes ago.
    Third Voice: How long has the man been waiting?

You will read:
    A. For a long time.
    B. For just a few minutes.
    C. A few minutes ago.
    D. In a while.

From the conversation you know that the correct answer is *B*. Now get ready to listen to the five conversations.

Number Six.
    Woman: Where are you going?
    Man: To the library.
    Third voice: What did the woman ask the man?

Number Six.
    Woman: Where are you going?
    Man: To the library.
    Third voice: What did the woman ask the man?

<pause 12 seconds>

Number Seven.
    Man: You'd better slow down.
    Woman: What's wrong?
    Man: It looks like an accident up ahead.
    Third voice: Where are the man and the woman?

Number Seven.
    Man: You'd better slow down.
    Woman: What's wrong?
    Man: It looks like an accident up ahead.
    Third voice: Where are the man and the woman?

<pause 12 seconds>

Number Eight.
    Woman: How did you get here?
    Man: Peter gave me a ride.
    Third voice: What did the woman want to know?

Number Eight.
    Woman: How did you get here?
    Man: Peter gave me a ride.
    Third voice: What did the woman want to know?

<pause 12 seconds>

Number Nine.
    Man: I wish this test were over. I'm really not looking forward to it.
    Woman: Well, by this time tomorrow, you will have finished it.
    Man: What does the man have to do?

Number Nine.
    Man: I wish this test were over. I'm really not looking forward to it.
    Woman: Well, by this time tomorrow, you will have finished it.
    Man: What does the man have to do?

<pause 12 seconds>

Number Ten.
    Woman: Are you leaving soon?
    Man: Yes, I am.
    Third Voice: What did the man say?

Number Ten.
    Woman: Are you leaving soon?
    Man: Yes, I am.
    Third Voice: What did the man say?

BOOK 2: TEST C
Answer Key

Part 1
1. C
2. A
3. D
4. B
5. D

Part 2
6. A
7. C
8. C
9. A
10. D

Part 3
11. Ted asked John if he had had any trouble finding it.
12. Jon said that he hadn't. *or* Jon said that he hadn't had any trouble finding it.
13. Tania asked Alex where the car was.
14. Alex said that he had parked it in back.
15. Stacey asked Marilyn when Jack had left.
16. Marilyn said that he had left before nine.
17. Kip asked if Tab was inside.
18. Sarah said that he wasn't.
19. Peter asked Josh if he knew where Anne had gone.
20. Josh said that he thought she had gone to the store.

Part 4
21. B
22. D
23. C
24. A
25. B
26. C
27. A
28. A
29. B
30. B

Part 5
31. where Jake is.
32. why the lights aren't working.
33. why he had gotten angry.
34. how long the movie is.
35. where the post office is.

Part 6
36. D
37. A
38. D
39. A
40. B

Part 7
41. B
42. C
43. A
44. B
45. D